'13

SONy

ABDO
Publishing Company

SONY

THE COMPANY AND ITS FOUNDERS

by Robert Grayson

Content Consultant
Chris Morris
Freelance Journalist, Technology Specialist
www.chrismorrisjournalist.com

CREDITS

Published by ABDO Publishing Company, PO Box 398166, Minneapolis, MN 55439. Copyright © 2013 by Abdo Consulting Group, Inc. International copyrights reserved in all countries. No part of this book may be reproduced in any form without written permission from the publisher. The Essential Library™ is a trademark and logo of ABDO Publishing Company.

Printed in the United States of America,
North Mankato, Minnesota
052012
092012

 THIS BOOK CONTAINS AT LEAST 10% RECYCLED MATERIALS.

Editor: Angela Wiechmann
Series Designer: Emily Love

Library of Congress Cataloging-in-Publication Data
Grayson, Robert, 1951-
  Sony : the company and its founders / Robert Grayson.
      p. cm. -- (Technology pioneers)
  Includes bibliographical references and index.
  ISBN 978-1-61783-335-9
  1. Morita, Akio, 1921-1999--Juvenile literature. 2. Industrialists-
-Japan--Biography--Juvenile literature. 3. Soni Kabushiki Kaisha-
-Juvenile literature. 4. Electronic industries--Japan--History--
Juvenile literature. I. Title.
  HD9696.A3J334627 2013
  338.4'76213810952--dc23
                                                    2012011528

TABLE OF CONTENTS

Sony chairman Akio Morita believed the Walkman would be a smash hit.

A SOUND IDEA

I t was the most popular tech gadget of its day. Called the Walkman, for lack of a better name, it was the almost accidental creation of Masaru Ibuka and Akio Morita, cofounders of Sony, an electronics and entertainment company. This portable audiocassette player with headphones was small enough to fit in a person's hand. But it was big enough to change the way the world listened to music. It would become synonymous with the Sony name.

One late February afternoon in 1979, Ibuka mentioned to chairman Morita how much he enjoyed listening to classical music on long flights across the Pacific. He said he used one of the company's portable tape recorders, a TC-D5, and a clunky pair of headphones. Ibuka loved the sound quality, but the TC-D5, which Sony released in 1978, was not easy to carry around. It was about the size of a hardcover book and weighed five pounds (2.3 kg) with batteries. The headphones were just as clunky.

Morita understood Ibuka's problem. Stereos were everywhere—in homes, restaurants, stores, and cars. But people needed an easier way to enjoy their own music on the go.

A PORTABLE TAPE PLAYER

On a whim, Morita ordered engineers to create a new product by modifying another one of the company's portable tape recorders, the Pressman. The Pressman, released in 1977, was originally designed for members of the press to record interviews. Morita asked Sony engineers to improve the Pressman's sound quality. He also instructed them to remove the recording capability, so it could play cassette tapes but not record on them. The new device had to be lightweight and small. In addition, it had to work with headphones that were stylish and lightweight. The chairman insisted on one more thing: the new device had to be affordable for young people.

This would be a relatively simple machine for Sony to make. The company was already well known for its tape recorders, transistor radios, and mini-televisions. Sony had also developed revolutionary technology that produced the most vivid images ever seen on color televisions.

Years later, Morita would admit that when it came to creating the Walkman, "Everybody gave me a hard time. It seemed as though nobody liked the idea."[1] Sony engineers wondered why anyone would buy the device if it could not record. Morita argued that millions of people enjoyed car stereos, which could not record, either. But that stereo had to stay in the car. In contrast, people could easily take the new Sony device anywhere. Morita was convinced millions would sell.

By February 1979, Sony's engineers placed a prototype of the device on Morita's desk. They called it a "walking stereo," complete with light, flexible headphones. Morita was ecstatic. He rushed home and played all kinds of music on it. His wife mentioned she wished she could listen to the device with him. So Morita made one small revision on the prototype, making room for two headphone jacks.

Ibuka loved the prototype as well. Morita ordered the company to put the device in full production within weeks.

CREATING A MARKET

Ibuka was always fond of saying that the genius behind Sony's market research for the Walkman was that they did not do any research at all. Morita explained,

CAUGHT ON TAPE

Vinyl records were the standard form of recorded music in the 1940s through the early 1960s. Then in 1962, the Netherlands-based Philips Company developed an audiocassette, a small plastic container with recording tape inside it. Philips marketed its audiocassettes for recording business meetings and notes. But Polygram Records, a subsidiary of Philips, had a different idea—to record music on the cassettes. Tapes, as they were sometimes called, grew in popularity during the 1970s as a more portable alternative to vinyl records. And then with the popularity of the Walkman, audiocassette tapes finally outsold vinyl records in 1983.

GUARANTEED SUCCESS

Sony employees were shocked in the spring of 1979 when Morita instructed them to manufacture 30,000 Walkman units. This was before the public had even heard of the product. At the time, the company's best tape recorder was selling only 15,000 units a month. Morita was so sure the 30,000 units would sell, he said he would resign as company chairman if they did not. Since then, more than 200 million Walkman units have been sold.

The public does not know what is possible, but we do. So instead of doing a lot of market research, we refine our thinking on a product and its use and try to create a market by educating and communicating with the public. . . . I do not believe that any amount of market research could have told us that the Sony Walkman would be successful.[2]

While Morita was excited, his marketing department was not. But the chairman, who had already made a name for himself with his savvy marketing skills, did not let that stop him. He was already working on a promotional campaign for this new product. But first, it needed a name.

The original idea was to call it a Stereo Walky, but Toshiba, another electronics company, was using the name Walky for its portable radios. The next idea was

Walkman, a play on Sony's Pressman tape recorders. Nobody liked it. Sony's marketing team worried the word *walkman* was improper English and thought it would never catch on worldwide. But the company was about to unveil the product to the press on June 22, 1979. It would hit retail stores in Japan by July 1. There was no time to think up a better idea, so Sony went with Walkman.

When Sony introduced the Walkman to the press, the marketing event made as many headlines as the product itself. The company drove members of the media to Yoyogi Park, one of Tokyo's largest recreation areas. Each reporter was given a Walkman to try out while walking amid lush trees in the park. The cassette tape in

ALL IN A NAME

Unhappy with the name Walkman, the Sony marketing department proposed selling the product under different names in different countries. They were set to package it as the Stowaway in England, Freestyle in Australia, and Soundabout in the United States. But just as distribution was about to begin in November 1979, Morita decided the world should know the new product under one name—Walkman.

Morita acknowledged in the mid-1980s that people often thought the name Walkman was inspired. But he admitted he never liked it. When reporters asked how to refer to more than one Walkman, Sony responded with a press release stating the plural is Walkman Personal Stereos, rather than Walkmans or Walkmen.

In 1986, Sony received the ultimate honor of having the word *Walkman* included in the *Oxford English Dictionary*, making it an official part of the English language.

each Walkman contained a pitch for the product, complete with background music.

As the reporters toured the park, young Sony employees and hired models passed by, listening to Walkman players while jogging, walking dogs, or riding bicycles, skateboards, and roller skates. It was a fitting introduction to what would become a worldwide symbol of youth and vibrancy.

Morita continued building the entire promotional campaign around style, fashion, sportiness, and youthful exuberance. Even after the press event at the park, he hired young people to listen to Walkman players while out and about in Tokyo and other Japanese cities. He instructed them to let curious people listen to the players.

The first 30,000 units sold out by the end of August 1979, a month after the first Walkman hit shelves in Japan. It was a

WORLDWIDE BUZZ

Early Walkman promotions in Japan had worldwide impact. In the summer of 1979, foreign businesspeople, airline crews, and tourists saw people walking around Tokyo with the sleek new device. Once they listened to the Walkman, they had to have it. When they returned home, all their friends wanted to know where they could get one. By November, Morita was getting calls about the Walkman from friends in France, England, Germany, and the United States.

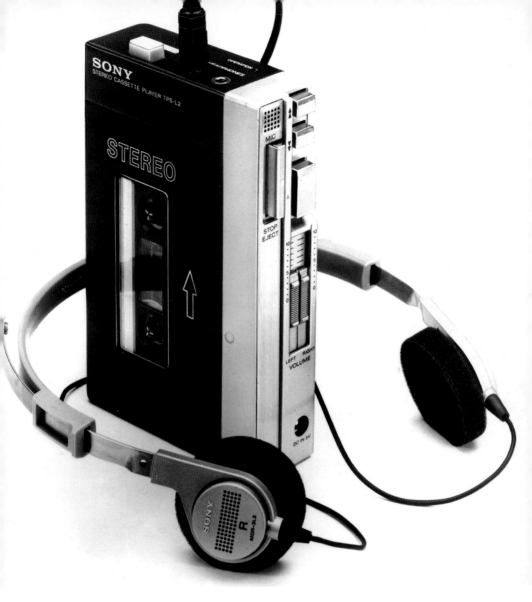

The Walkman delivered high-quality sound in a portable size.

smash hit. So many young people had to have a
Sony Walkman that Japanese retailers could hardly
keep enough in stock. Orders doubled the next

LIVING LARGE

In the late 1970s, before the Walkman, boom boxes were all the rage when it came to portable cassette players. The bigger the better—these music players were one to three feet (30.5 to 91 cm) wide and weighed ten to fifteen pounds (4.5 to 6.8 kg). People carried them atop one shoulder, "booming" music in public for all to hear. It was hardly a private sound system like the Walkman, but the boom box was still quite popular with music lovers.

month and then tripled. By early 1980, the Sony Walkman was an international phenomenon.

Sony's worldwide popularity as an electronics manufacturer skyrocketed. What would the company do for an encore? +

The Walkman allowed people to enjoy their music on the go.

Sony founders Masaru Ibuka, *right*, and Akio Morita each had a love for technology and innovation.

BORN TO INVENT

orn April 11, 1908, in Nikko City, Japan, Masaru Ibuka first experienced "the excitement of putting things together" when he received an Erector set toy in second grade.[1] Throughout his life, he never lost that youthful exuberance for making new and innovative things. As a teenager, he built his own ham radio, a type of hobby radio used for amateur broadcasting. While attending the School of Science and Engineering at Waseda University in Tokyo, Ibuka earned the nickname "genius inventor." Among other things, he built a loudspeaker system for the athletic field and an electric phonograph so he could listen to records in his spare time.

EARLY SUCCESS

Not long after he graduated from college in 1933, Ibuka received public attention for one of his inventions. He developed a light-transmission system that could control the brightness of light. He called it "dancing neon." He entered the product in the Paris Exhibition, an international science fair, in 1933. He won the highest honor, a Gold Prize. His triumph made headlines in all the Tokyo newspapers.

MR. FIX-IT

Ibuka was a relentless tinkerer. He loved to fix things rather than throw them away. It was a challenge to him, and he never missed an opportunity to make repairs. It was not unusual for someone to walk into the Sony founder's office and see him toying with an old radio or watch. He would often call out to Morita in a neighboring office to see if he had a particular tool needed to complete a repair.

Later the same year, the inventor considered a job at Tokyo Shibaura Electric Company, known today as Toshiba. Ibuka failed the screening exam because he was so wrapped up in his own ideas. But he soon found work at Photo-Chemical Laboratory. The company's owner, Taiji Uemura, personally guaranteed Ibuka would have the freedom to pursue his own technological interests.

While Japan was engaged in World War II (1939–1945), Ibuka convinced Uemura to start a new company. It would be solely devoted to researching and developing technology used to fight wars, from radar detection and telephone scramblers to weaponry. Called Japan Measuring Instruments, the new company thrived under Ibuka's leadership, selling its inventions to the Japanese military.

In 1944, even with Japan facing certain defeat in the war, Ibuka became involved in a project with the Wartime Research Committee at the Yokosuka Naval Base. He was not in the military himself, but other committee members belonged to the army and navy. There Ibuka met a young navy lieutenant named Akio Morita. The two men forged an almost instant bond, even though Ibuka was 13 years older than the young, brash naval officer. Morita was captivated by Ibuka's technical knowledge.

FASCINATED BY HOW THINGS WORK

Morita was born on January 26, 1921, to a wealthy and very traditional family in Nagoya, a city in central Japan. Morita was the firstborn child, and his parents planned for him to follow tradition and take over the family's centuries-old sake brewery. Sake is a rice-based alcoholic beverage that has been popular in Japan and other countries for hundreds of years. But even as a young child, Morita showed other interests, especially technology, that would lead him away from the family business.

By the time he reached elementary school, the young Morita was curious about how everyday appliances worked. He would go around his home

HOBBIES

Morita and Ibuka were fascinated with technology even outside their work. Morita collected player pianos and mechanical organs. Ibuka was an avid collector of model trains and was even president of the Japan Association of Microtrains. His hobby spilled over into the workplace: he had a small train track mounted on the wall of his office.

taking things apart and putting them back together. To help satisfy this curiosity, Morita enjoyed reading the manuals that came with appliances and toys.

Morita's father noticed his son's interests strayed from the path of the family business, but he did not discourage him. With his father's consent, Morita entered a science program in high school. Akio's younger brother Kazuaki later recalled, "At some point, I began to wonder if my brother really intended to take over the business as Father expected."[2]

Upon entering Osaka Imperial University in 1940, Morita chose physics over business and economics. Although disappointed, Morita's father gave him permission to pursue science. He appeared to have accepted that his eldest son was not ready to carry on the family tradition.

The Japanese war effort came to an end as Japan formally surrendered to the Allied forces on September 2, 1945.

Shortly after graduating from college in 1944, Morita received his draft notice to enter the Japanese military and take up arms in World War II. Morita had no interest in the military, but he had little

RISKY BUSINESS

The postwar economy in Japan was in shambles. There was high unemployment, and food was hard to come by. That made Ibuka's decision to leave his job at Japan Measuring Instruments and start a new business even more shocking to his colleagues. But once Ibuka made a decision, there was no changing his mind. He made the risky move without a second thought.

choice in the matter. With his physics degree, Morita was sent to the Naval Office of Aviation Technology at the Yokosuka base. There he met Ibuka, who was headquartered at the base with the Wartime Research Committee.

Japan announced its intention to surrender to the United States and the other Allied powers on August 15, 1945, and World War II ended. As he contemplated what he would do next, Morita realized he might eventually have to take over the family business. But with his father still running the company, enjoying good health and showing no signs of slowing down, Morita felt there was time to pursue a job teaching physics.

LAUNCHING A NEW VENTURE

Once the war ended, Ibuka became convinced Japan Measuring Instruments was not equipped to succeed in a peacetime economy. When he announced he was starting a business of his own, seven of the engineers volunteered to go with him.

In early October 1945, they opened a radio repair business on the third floor of a bombed-out department store in a once-bustling district of Tokyo. The company was called Tokyo Telecommunications Research Laboratories (which was also known as Tokyo Telecommunications Research Institute). The new activity in the charred building caught the attention of a newspaper reporter, who wrote an article about Ibuka's small company.

RADIO DAYS

While many people saw only the hard work it would take to rebuild Japan's cities and economy after World War II, Ibuka saw opportunities. He saw a chance to have an impact and contribute to his country's future. With that in mind, he thought opening a radio repair business in a bombed-out area would bring hope to the people of his nation.

Ibuka's new business offered a vital service. Radios had been very important to the Japanese people during World War II. Radios had broadcasted air-raid warnings and other critical information. After the war, people still valued their radios. They wanted to repair them and keep them in top condition because, like most things in postwar Japan, new radios were hard to come by.

But the business did more than just repair radios. Ibuka also developed an adapter that allowed regular AM radios to pick up shortwave broadcasts worldwide. The adapter became very popular as it gave the average Japanese citizen access to programming from other countries. The company also developed an electric rice cooker. The new invention was innovative, but the technology was not quite perfect. It did not sell.

Shortly after taking a teaching job at the Tokyo Institute of Technology, Morita saw the newspaper article about his wartime friend's new business. It seemed as though both men were seeking fresh starts. Before the end of October, Morita contacted Ibuka, who was overjoyed to hear from him. The two men met, talked for hours, and set in motion a plan to go into business together. +

Morita and Ibuka embarked on their business venture as Japan began
reconstructing its postwar economy.

In 1997, Empress Michiko, *right*, and Princess Sayako inspected the tape recorders that helped launch Japan's electronics field.

RISING FROM THE RUINS

Following Japanese tradition, Morita had to convince his father to release him from his obligation to run the family's sake company before he could join Ibuka in their new business venture. In April 1946, the two prospective partners took a train trip from Tokyo to the Morita family home in Kosugaya to meet with Morita's father, Kyuzaemon.

After a long meeting, Morita's father, a rather conservative man, agreed to let his eldest son go out on his own. For the first time in 14 generations, the eldest son would not be running the Morita family company. Kazuaki, the next oldest son, would now be expected to take over the company. Kazuaki called the decision "a huge event."[1]

Kyuzaemon seemed intrigued by the start-up venture his son and Ibuka talked about. He even agreed to invest what amounts to approximately $60,000 today in the new enterprise. It would not be the last time Morita's father would provide financial support for the fledgling business, each time getting stock in return.

On May 7, 1946, Ibuka and Morita launched

SOLID BACKING

Many people launched businesses in post-World War II Japan, but few survived. New companies need a lot of capital. There was very little available at the time. But Ibuka had connections through his father-in-law, a former government official. He introduced Ibuka to bankers and wealthy investors. Morita's father had contacts as well. Those contacts were especially interested in backing Tokyo Telecommunications Engineering Corporation after Morita's father invested some of the family fortune in it.

CORPORATE PHILOSOPHY

On May 7, 1946, Ibuka and Morita held a ceremony to launch their new business. Ibuka read from the company's founding prospectus: "The first and primary motive for setting up this company was to create a stable work environment where engineers who had a deep and profound appreciation for technology could realize their societal mission and work to their heart's content."[3] That remains the company's philosophy to this day.

their new business, Tokyo Telecommunications Engineering Corporation. It was called Tokyo Tsushin Kogyo in Japanese—Totsuko for short. The company would eventually change its name to Sony in 1958. Ibuka was named president and Morita vice president. The new venture incorporated Ibuka's radio repair business and its entire staff. But the new company would do more than repair radios. Ibuka and Morita wanted to make their own products. To stand out in the marketplace, they would have to come up with ingenious, innovative products. "I had often spoken of the concept of our new company as an innovator, a clever company that would make new technology products in ingenious ways," Morita said.[2]

JAPAN'S FIRST TAPE RECORDER

By 1949, engineers at Tokyo Telecommunications Engineering Corporation were working on a promising project both Ibuka and Morita enthusiastically supported. The company was focusing on producing tape recorders to record speech, music, and other sound. German engineers had developed reel-to-reel tape recorders in the 1930s and used them during World War II. US engineers had produced some as well. For the most part, governments and businesses used the recorders. Very few people purchased them for home use. Ibuka and Morita wanted to create a top-quality tape recorder for everyday use. Ibuka and his team of engineers built many prototypes and did extensive testing. But none of them met the standards of excellence the company set. So work continued on the recorder.

HOT IDEA

Before the tape recorders, one of the earliest products Ibuka and Morita developed was a heated area rug, similar to a modern-day heating pad. It was perfect to spread out and sit on during a cold winter's day. The public liked the product, and it sold well. It had no thermostat to control the temperature, however. Ibuka worried the rug could catch fire, much as a competitor's product had. He decided to stop manufacturing it shortly after it hit the market in 1947.

Right from the start, Ibuka and Morita decided they not only wanted to make tape recorders. They also wanted to corner the whole market by producing the recording tape used in the machines. People would need to buy both products from them. Recording tape is a long, narrow, thin strip of material, looped through a recorder. The tape is treated with a magnetic material, such as iron oxide, that allows it to record sound.

While some engineers worked on developing the recorders, another team worked on creating the recording tape. It was even tougher to develop than the recorder itself. Finding the right material was a major problem for the Tokyo Telecommunications Engineering Corporation team. Cellophane did not work because it stretched and distorted the sound. Plastic, which was used to make recording tape in the United States and Germany, was impossible to find in Japan after World War II. And most paper was too thin.

Finally, Morita went to see one of his cousins who worked for Honshu Paper Company in Osaka. Morita asked if the company could produce a craft paper that was extra smooth and very strong. Back at Tokyo Telecommunications Engineering Corporation, employees painstakingly coated the paper with a paste made from magnetic powder so it could be used to record sound. As with the tape recorder, efforts to perfect the recording tape failed several times before it produced the sound quality the inventors wanted.

In January 1950, Ibuka and Morita proudly introduced Japan's first tape recorder, complete with recording tape. They had so much confidence in their new products, the two entrepreneurs were not sure if they could handle all the orders. But as Morita recalled,

> *We were in for a rude awakening. The tape recorder was so new to Japan that almost no one knew what a tape recorder was, and most of the people*

MUTUAL RESPECT

Engineers worked hard to develop the high-quality tape recorder Ibuka wanted. They did it partly out of determination, but mostly out of respect for their boss and a desire to please him. Ibuka had a strong personal connection with his engineers. Mechanical engineer Nobutoshi Kihara worked with Ibuka on more than 700 patented products. He believed Ibuka truly understood the mind of an engineer. Kihara said,

> *He never instructed me to do anything. Instead of ordering, he'd discuss things with you and make suggestions—he'd tell you what he hoped for. To all of us, that was a very special gift. When you receive an order, you have to do what you've been told. But I was always like Ibuka, I hated imitating others.*[4]

The engineer recalled when Ibuka was overjoyed with a prototype. "'Kihara, this is just what I wanted!' he'd say. . . . He was like a happy kid at those moments, and I'd love seeing him that way."[5]

who did know could not see why they should buy one. It was not something people felt they needed.[6]

MARKETING SAVVY

The tape recorders were not selling. While company engineers became discouraged, Morita became more determined. He launched a campaign to convince Japanese people they needed tape recorders. It would be the first of many displays of his dynamic marketing skills.

Morita went with a team of salespeople to pitch the tape recorders at government agencies. They demonstrated how the device could record meetings. Court administrators were impressed. Ibuka and Morita also went to grade schools, high schools, and universities. The men showed how the tape recorder could be

TRUE GRIT

Just how dedicated were Ibuka, Morita, and their employees to developing recording tape? After Morita finally found the right material to make the tape, the next problem was that they could not find the right machine to apply the magnetic paste to it. So, employees laid the paper out on the factory floor. Everybody—company owners too—got on their hands and knees and applied the paste by hand with small paintbrushes.

Tokyo Telecommunications Engineering Corporation salespeople
convinced schools they needed tape recorders.

used to enhance learning. The schools bought many
units. Ibuka and Morita went to moviemakers and
convinced them to buy the tape recorders, too. All
the while, they gained publicity about their new
product. People were learning what a tape recorder
was all about.

Back at the company's offices, engineers were
working on a portable tape recorder that was less
expensive, lighter, smaller, and more user friendly

for the average person. The P-Type portable tape recorder hit store shelves in mid-1951. Tape recorders were making the company money. Slowly but surely, Tokyo Telecommunications Engineering Corporation was gaining the recognition it needed to make a big impact in the technology field. +

Mechanical engineer Nobutoshi Kihara displays the P-Type portable tape recorder that put the company on the road to success.

Ibuka knew the success of his company depended on the transistor radio.

SMALL WONDER

As 1952 approached, Tokyo Telecommunications Engineering Corporation had established a solid market in Japan for tabletop tape recorders and recording tape, as well as lightweight portable recorders. With their success in Japan,

Ibuka and Morita were curious about how recording technology was being used in the United States.

In March 1952, the two men traveled to New York City to see what they could learn. Ibuka contacted Bell Laboratories about some interesting research being done there. In 1947, scientists at the US company had invented the transistor, a small device that controls the flow of electricity throughout a machine or appliance. At the time, vacuum tubes served the same function in radios and other appliances, including the tape recorders made at Tokyo Telecommunications Engineering Corporation. Compared to vacuum tubes, transistors were less expensive, smaller, and more reliable. Now the transistor was set to revolutionize the field of electronics.

Ibuka found out that Bell Laboratories' parent company, Western Electric, was offering a license for the transistor. Licensing the transistor would mean the Japanese company could reproduce it and use it in its own products.

ON THE MOVE

In 1947, a few years before the Tokyo Telecommunications Engineering Corporation developed the transistor radio, the company moved from its old offices in the burned-out ruins of a Tokyo department store. They set up shop in a wooden factory building in the southern part of Tokyo. Sony's worldwide headquarters stands on the site today.

Ibuka looked into licensing the transistor for Tokyo Telecommunications Engineering Corporation and began laying the groundwork for the company's next major project. The small transistor fascinated him. "[Ibuka] didn't know just then what we would make with the transistor if we got the technology, but he was excited by the technological breakthrough it represented," Morita said.[1]

Engineers at Bell Laboratories had not explored using the transistor in consumer electronics. They felt the transistor would work best in hearing aids, and they also considered using it for military equipment. But Ibuka and Morita thought the transistor could have the most impact in products for everyday use. Ibuka and Morita believed their company—made up of talented, committed, and well-educated engineers—was the perfect place to push this latest technology to its limit. As they flew home, the two men talked about using the transistor to make smaller electronic products that would use less power. The Japanese culture admired things that were compact.

Their first objective was to use the transistor in a miniature radio a person could carry in a pocket or purse, called a transistor radio. At the time, speakers for radios and sound systems were getting bigger.

Some engineers thought using a lot of vacuum tubes produced the best sound. However, that required larger speaker boxes to hold those cumbersome, bulky tubes. The transistor radio was a new direction.

By August 1953, Ibuka and Morita had a license for the transistor. Things were falling into place.

PAINSTAKING WORK

Once the license was secured, engineers at Tokyo Telecommunications Engineering Corporation could work with the transistor and make improvements. They made it more powerful for use in consumer electronics. This was complicated and painstaking work—something the engineers in the United States had not been able to accomplish. At the same time, the company worked to make other

COMPETITION

Ibuka and Morita wanted to produce the world's first transistor radio, but Regency, a US company, beat them to the marketplace by a month. Regency made a transistor radio about the same size as the TR-55. They used transistors developed by a company called Texas Instruments. However, Regency felt there was no future in the "novelty" product. They put no effort into marketing it and eventually gave up on it.

The Sony TR-55 transistor radio, first launched in 1955, was an audio marvel.

scaled-down radio parts to match the small size of the transistor.

Most important of all was the company's goal to use the transistor in a high-quality product that would be respected throughout the world. Because many Japanese companies struggled after World War II, some people felt the label "Made in Japan" symbolized less expensive, poorly made versions of US products. Ibuka and Morita wanted their new transistor radios to be the envy of the electronics field worldwide.

Meanwhile, Ibuka and Morita decided the only way the company could grow was to sell its products outside Japan. But to do this, the partners realized the products needed a brand name that was shorter and easier to remember than Tokyo Telecommunications Engineering Corporation. After much debate, the two entrepreneurs decided on the name Sony. They began using the Sony name and logo on their products in 1955, and eventually in 1958, they made it their company's name.

In August 1955, Sony released the TR-55, Japan's first transistor radio. At a nifty 5.5 inches tall, 3.5 inches wide, and 1.5 inches thick (14 cm by 8.9 cm by 3.85 cm), it was roughly the size of a wallet. Though it was a bit bigger than Ibuka and Morita wanted, Japanese consumers marveled at this compact audio wonder. Immediately after the

MELTING MESS

Before the TR-55, Sony developed the TR-52 radio. It had a white plastic lattice piece on its front. It looked stylish. But right before the company could preview this new product with the press, disaster struck. It was summer, and the hot temperature made the lattice piece melt and peel off on nearly every one of their 100 preliminary units. Ibuka and Morita had to call off the launch, abandon the faulty product, and start over with a new model. They made sure their next transistor radio, the TR-55, was durable as well as stylish.

launch of the TR-55, the company's engineers began working feverishly to come up with an even smaller transistor radio.

In the fall of 1955, Morita took some of the company's products to New York City to make inroads in the US market. Morita quickly managed to arrange a meeting with the purchasing agent for the well-established Bulova Watch Company. The agent loved the TR-55 transistor radio and shocked Morita by placing an order for 100,000 units on the spot. There was only one catch: the radios had to be sold under the Bulova name.

Morita insisted on using the Sony brand name. He felt the radios would help establish the Sony brand in the United States, which he

A NEW NAME

The name Tokyo Telecommunications Engineering Corporation was too long to put on products. Totsuko was rather forgettable and hard to pronounce outside Japan. So, Ibuka and Morita set out to find a brand name people would remember. They knew it was the only way to build a customer following outside their homeland, especially in the United States. "We wanted a new name that could be recognized anywhere in the world, one that could be pronounced in any language. We made dozens and dozens of tries," Morita recalled.[2]

Finally, they came across the Latin word *sonus*, which means "sound." They were also aware that some people in Japan were using the US slang *sonny*. It referred to bright young men, such as those at Ibuka and Morita's company. "The answer struck me one day: why not just drop one of the letters and make it 'Sony'? That was it!" Morita said.[3]

thought was vital to the company's growth. Bulova refused to budge on its demand. Though Morita's colleagues, including Ibuka, begged him to take the order, he turned it down.

With the Bulova deal dead, Morita turned to an old friend from Japan, Shido Yamada, who now worked and lived in New York City. Yamada introduced Morita to Adolph Gross, an importer who had plenty of contacts in the retail market throughout the United States. He was impressed with the transistor radio and offered to get it distributed to stores in the United States under the Sony brand. Reassured that he had done the right thing in turning down the Bulova deal, Morita told Ibuka about Gross's proposal. They signed a five-year deal with Gross.

The first product the company sold in the United States was the TR-63 pocket-size transistor radio.

WHAT A STEAL!

In mid-January 1958, thieves broke into a Sony distributor's warehouse in New York. They stole 4,000 TR-63 radios. The warehouse contained electronic products from other manufacturers as well. But the thieves took only the Sony radios. The theft made big headlines, especially in the *New York Times*. Consumers reasoned that if the crooks left all the other merchandise behind, it must mean the Sony product was highly sought after. Sales of the pocket-size Sony radios soared after the heist.

The TR-63 was much smaller than the TR-55. In fact, the TR-63 was the smallest radio ever made up until that time. Released in March 1957, it measured 4.25 inches tall, 2.75 inches wide, and 1.25 inches thick (11.2 cm by 7.1 cm by 3.2 cm). It had great reception, it was powered by a small battery, and it could be used with an earphone. The new product captivated customers, who were mesmerized by its size and its crystal-clear sound. It came in different colors, and it had the Sony name on the front. The pocket-size radio eventually sold 1.5 million units.

Morita often said turning down the Bulova order was the best business decision he ever made. The Sony brand was now a household name worldwide. +

As Sony's products became more popular, more workers were needed to assemble the very tiny transistors.

In the late 1950s and early 1960s, Sony turned its attention to televisions, launching many groundbreaking products, such as the TV5-303 in 1962.

A BETTER TELEVISION

Thanks to transistor radio sales, Ibuka and Morita's once-small business was worth $2.5 million and had 1,200 employees by the end of 1957. In January 1958, Tokyo Telecommunications Engineering Corporation officially changed its name to Sony. The growing electronics firm was ready for a new challenge.

Sony was quickly establishing itself as an innovative leader in the electronics field. With the pocket-size transistor radio, Sony launched the microelectronics industry, which focused on creating smaller and smaller electronic products. When people saw the quality of Sony's radio line, they began realizing products from Japan could be well made and long lasting. The company helped make Japan the worldwide leader in transistor radio production.

PORTABLE TELEVISIONS

Now Sony found another way to expand its product line. It used the transistor to make a truly portable television. There were "portable" televisions on the market at the time, but at roughly 40 pounds (18 kg), they were too heavy to realistically take on the go. The tubes inside the televisions made them weigh so much. Ibuka wanted to make a black-and-white

SONY SIZE

Sony's mini-televisions stood apart from the US trend for big, heavy television sets in large consoles, or cabinets. The mini-televisions meant people could watch programs not just in the living room, but in the kitchen, the bedroom, and even outdoors. People started referring to any small electronics as "Sony size." The company took that description as a compliment to its innovation.

television with a transistor. He wanted it to be lightweight, with a small eight-inch (23 cm) screen and clear reception. The team started working on the project in September 1958. It would be Sony's first foray into the television market.

A television—even a small one—required a much more sophisticated transistor than a radio did. The engineers realized they would have to completely redevelop the transistor. The team did a lot of experimenting and had several failures until they produced a transistor that could do the job. It took approximately a year. Then it was on to building the actual television set.

CALCULATING

Sony used transistors in more than just radios and televisions. In March 1964, Sony engineers unveiled the world's first desktop calculator with a transistor. They demonstrated it to an amazed crowd at the 1964 World's Fair in New York City. But Sony got out of the calculator business in the late 1960s when many other Japanese companies began making calculators too.

In May 1960, the groundbreaking TV8-301 television with an eight-inch screen was ready to hit the market. It weighed approximately eight pounds (4 kg). It contained 23 transistors and could run on either electricity or batteries. The pint-size television cost Sony a lot to produce, and the production cost

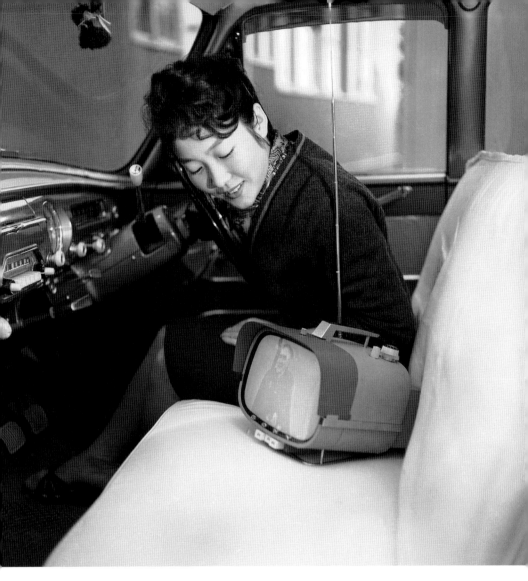

Sony's mini-televisions allowed people to take television out of the living room and into new places, such as their cars.

was reflected in the price tag when the television was released. It cost $250 (approximately $1,900 today), while larger 27-inch (68.5 cm) black-and-white televisions sold for just $150. Despite the price, the mini-television sold well. It was a luxury item. Those who could afford it loved it.

In 1962, Sony introduced the TV5-303. It was a bit lighter and had a five-inch (12.5 cm) screen. It was nicknamed the "Tummy Television" because people could rest it nicely on their stomachs when watching television in bed at night. By 1969, Sony had sold more than 1 million mini-televisions. The company continued expanding its grasp on the microelectronics market.

Even as they sold the small black-and-white televisions, dealers were asking Sony's sales division when the company was coming out with a color model. The salespeople then pressured management. But the Sony founders were reluctant to produce color televisions.

LIVING COLOR

In the early 1960s, black-and-white televisions outsold color sets by a 50-to-1 margin in the United States. Images were dark and murky on color televisions of the time. Ibuka reasoned that consumers did not want to pay high prices for poor quality. He refused to use what he considered inferior technology in Sony products. "We will only do great products. We will only do high quality products. We will only do breakthrough technology," Ibuka said.[1] Ibuka felt color television should be vivid, vibrant, and true to life.

Then in March 1961, the Sony founders were attending an electronics trade show in New York City. There they saw a demonstration of a picture tube, a device that displays onscreen images, that produced much brighter color images than they had ever seen. The technology, called Chromatron, had been developed for the US military. Morita was impressed and instantly went to work licensing the

COMING TO AMERICA

While Ibuka focused on improving Sony's technology, Morita was focused on improving its business. He felt Sony could make 50 percent of its revenue selling overseas. But Sony, like all other Japanese companies, had little control over how its products were sold and distributed in the United States. So, he established Sony Corporation of America, also called SONAM, on February 15, 1960, to handle distribution, marketing, and sales in the United States. Morita said the goal was "doing business with Americans like an American company."[2]

The move was a bold one. No other Japanese company had ever tried it. Sony hired US managers to run SONAM, though Morita remained its president until 1966. Eventually, Sony would open subsidiaries in other countries.

Sony made another business breakthrough in the United States on June 7, 1961, this time in the stock market. The company sold 2 million shares of common stock on the New York Stock Exchange. That marked the first time a Japanese company traded on the exchange. Sony raised $3 million in capital through the sale to help the company grow.

SELLING CHROMATRON

Sony engineers had been so sure the Chromatron technology would work, they had an assembly plant ready and waiting to mass-produce the televisions. But due to the high manufacturing costs, Sony made only approximately 13,000 sets. Though the sets cost $1,000 each to make, they each sold for only $500. Sony hoped to eventually find a way to drop manufacturing costs so Chromatron would bring in a profit. It never happened. Thankfully, Sony had gone in a new direction and developed the Trinitron technology instead, to great success.

technology. Two years later, Sony had a prototype for a color television using the cutting-edge Chromatron technology.

Mass-producing the Chromatron color televisions, however, proved to be slow and expensive. It cost Sony roughly $1,000 to build one television set, and the company could make only 1,000 sets per month. In comparison, RCA, another electronics company, was building 25,000 color sets per month. RCA also produced each set at a much lower cost than Sony could.

Sony had spent a lot of money in the hopes of turning the Chromatron technology into the best color television ever made. But after four years, the company still had not found an affordable way to mass-produce color televisions. These were tense times at the company. Some people at Sony wanted to give up on color television. But Ibuka pressed on.

ANOTHER TRY

In fall 1966, Ibuka assembled Sony's top 30 engineers and instructed them to "start looking for a process to replace Chromatron." He added, "This time I will act as team leader from start to finish."[3] Working day and night, they explored every possible solution to create their own color television technology.

Finally, in October 1967, the team found the answer. They developed a technology that produced even brighter, crisper, and sharper images than Chromatron. It was also simple to mass-produce. The picture on their prototype was 25 percent clearer than that of any color television in existence at that time. Called Trinitron, the technology was so revolutionary that it would earn Sony an Emmy Award in May 1973. It was the first product to ever win television's highest honor, usually given only to shows and actors.

In October 1968, the portable Trinitron television hit the shelves with a 12-inch (30.5 cm) screen. From there, the line grew to include bigger

QUITE A DEMONSTRATION

Sony was always working on new products, even as the televisions hit the market. Morita showed off Sony's latest invention—a video camera recorder, a forerunner of today's camcorder—at the 1964 World's Fair in New York City. As Morita was talking, a fire broke out in the exhibit hall basement. Morita grabbed the video camera and ran to the fire, bringing along a *New York Times* reporter who had been in the crowd. Morita captured the fire on film. He then played it back for the spellbound journalist.

screens as well. Sony had a patent on the Trinitron technology until 1996. During that time, it was unsurpassed in color television quality, because the company kept making improvements to the Trinitron technology each year.

As soon as Sony's color televisions hit the market in 1968, Ibuka moved on to the next project. Now it was time to take video recording to a new level. +

From transistor mini-televisions to Trinitron color sets, Sony was a leader in the television market.

The popularity of video rentals in the 1980s fueled the VCR format war between Betamax and VHS.

VIDEO WAR

B y the early 1970s, Sony was unmatched when it came to making color televisions. However, Ibuka, who became Sony's chairman in 1971, had his sights set on another prize. He desperately wanted to develop a home video recorder. It would let people record their favorite television shows and play them back whenever they wanted. Ibuka had been thinking about this kind of device since the mid-1950s. He was determined to make it happen.

In 1962, a group of Sony engineers had developed the PV-100, the world's first all-transistor, black-and-white, reel-to-reel videotape recorder. It was compact for its time, but it still weighed approximately 125 pounds (57 kg). The unit was not small enough for everyday home use, which was Ibuka's goal. The PV-100 was followed in 1964 by the much smaller CV-2000, weighing 33 pounds (15 kg). It was geared for home use, but the bulk of its sales came from educational and industrial markets.

Ibuka thought the video recorder needed some revisions in order to make it popular in living rooms around the world. He felt it had to record in both black-and-white and color. He also thought it had to use cassette tapes rather than reel-to-reel. Kihara, the leader of the team that developed the CV-2000, was flustered about the concept of a videocassette recorder (VCR). "The construction of a VCR is very complex. It will be extremely difficult to build a machine that will use a cassette tape, let alone in color," Kihara told Ibuka.[1] But Ibuka simply insisted

VIDEO "ON DEMAND"

Long before today's streaming media became a reality, seeing a movie "on demand" meant renting a video. VCRs brought movies into people's homes in the late 1970s, and video rentals were booming in the 1980s. VCR videos remained popular until the late 1990s, when digital video discs (DVDs) allowed people to watch movies at home with higher picture and sound quality. DVD players started replacing VCRs. Around the same time, digital video recorders (DVRs) were invented. DVRs allowed consumers to digitally record television programs, including on-demand movies, on a hard drive and play them back later.

it could be done. "Look how easy audio tape recorders can be used thanks to the cassette tape. Why can't we incorporate this function into video players?" Ibuka said.[2]

Kihara was not only designing a VCR, but also the videocassette tapes to go with it. His team made and discarded many VCR prototypes. They failed with several attempts to make the videotape cassettes as well. Success finally came in late 1969 when the team unveiled the prototype for the U-matic video recorder with tape cassette.

Sony's U-matic VP-1100 went on sale in 1971. It did not make its way into many homes. But it became an instant hit in television newsrooms across the United States. Producers found they could broadcast news faster by using U-matic video instead

Although Sony's Betamax, first released in 1975, was the first VCR on the market, it would eventually lose out to the rival VHS technology.

of reel-to-reel film. Still, the goal at Sony was to make a home video recorder.

BETAMAX DEBUTS

After four years of hard work, Sony introduced the world to Betamax, a home-use VCR, at a press conference on April 16, 1975. The device went on sale to the public on May 10. One of the first Betamax units was packaged with a Trinitron color television in a wooden cabinet. The Betamax

VAMP IT UP

When Betamax first came out, Sony aired television commercials featuring Count Dracula. In the ad, Dracula comes home to a dark apartment, puts on his Betamax recorder, and says, "If you work nights, like I do, you miss a lot of great TV programs. But I don't miss them anymore, thanks to Sony's Betamax deck, which hooks up to any TV set."[3]

recorder included in this unit was capable of recording one program while the viewer watched a different program at the same time. That function made the combined unit very popular, even at $2,300 (approximately $9,700 today). Each Betamax cassette was the size of a small paperback book, roughly 4 inches by 7 inches (10 by 18 cm). The blank tapes cost an additional $16 each. In 1976, Sony released a Betamax unit designed to fit easily on a shelf under a television or on top of a television cabinet. Sales were brisk for this model, even though the units cost roughly $1,300 apiece (roughly $5,200 today).

Having seen the VCR become a reality, Ibuka retired as Sony chairman in 1976. He became Sony's honorary chairman and still played an important role in the company. Ibuka handed the reins of power over to Morita. For decades, Morita had focused his attention on Sony's business operations. But now he had the dual role of overseeing the company's technological innovations as well. It would not be an easy task, since Betamax had a rough road ahead.

A CHALLENGE TO BETAMAX

Sony wanted all electronics companies to use the Betamax format for any home VCR they would produce. Sony had managed to make a similar arrangement with other companies when the U-matic format arrived in 1971. This time, Sony proposed to license the Betamax format to other companies that wanted to make home VCRs. Some companies, such as Sanyo and Toshiba, agreed. However, JVC,

THE CASE AGAINST BETAMAX

Not everyone was thrilled that VCRs let people record their favorite television shows at home. To show their displeasure, executives at Universal City Studios and Walt Disney Productions sued Sony on November 11, 1976, in US Federal District Court in Los Angeles, California. The film companies demanded Sony stop VCR sales, claiming that recording television programs broke copyright laws. Their complaint was that recording a show was like making an illegal copy of it.

The case went to trial on January 30, 1979. After five weeks of testimony, the court ruled in Sony's favor that taping a television show for viewing at a later time did not violate any copyright laws. Not giving up, the movie studios appealed the ruling, taking the case to a higher court. The US court of appeals reversed the lower court's decision in October 1981. Also not giving up, Sony took the case to the US Supreme Court—and won. By that time, 1.4 million VCRs were being sold yearly in the United States. On January 17, 1984, the Supreme Court proclaimed that taping a television show for private viewing in the future was considered fair use under copyright law. However, those taping the shows could not profit from them in any way.

BETAMOVIE

Betamax got a boost in May 1983 when Sony introduced Betamovie. It was the first camcorder for home movies. The camcorder recorded family movies on Betamax cassettes that could be played back instantly on a Betamax VCR. But later that same year, JVC released a camcorder for the VHS format. Betamax and VHS continued to lock horns in the video format war.

another Japanese electronics company, declined Sony's offer. JVC had been involved in the U-matic agreement. JVC management felt only Sony had benefited from that first deal and did not want Sony to capture this new market, too.

For a year, Sony basically had the home VCR market to itself. Then companies, most notably JVC, decided to develop a different home VCR format, recruiting the support of other Japanese electronics companies, including Matsushita (now known as Panasonic), Mitsubishi, and Sharp. In October 1976, JVC introduced its Video Home System (VHS) format in Japan. RCA's VHS systems reached the United States in 1977, and JVC's arrived in August 1978. The video format war was on.

The Betamax and VHS formats were not compatible.

VHS tapes did not work in a Betamax recorder, and vice versa. When shopping for a VCR, consumers had to choose one format or the other. Industry experts gave Betamax the edge in overall quality. But consumers liked VHS's longer-running tapes.

VHS started making inroads in the marketplace. VCRs using the VHS format cost approximately $300 less than Betamax machines, which was another key selling point. Sony lowered its price to try gaining more customers, but JVC went lower. Using the VHS format, more electronics companies, including Matsushita, produced VCRs of their own. As competition for sales heated up, VCR prices went down even more.

The war intensified when VCR movie rentals became popular in the early 1980s. People could rent movies to watch at home on their VCRs. At first, movie studios released tapes in both formats. But by 1981, Betamax had only 25 percent of the VCR sales in the United States. That led some

VHS TAPES GO THE DISTANCE

When deciding between Betamax and VHS, many consumers chose VHS simply because those tapes could record longer programs. Betamax tapes could hold only one hour of recording. They were fine for taping half-hour sitcoms or an hour-long drama. But they didn't work well for recording sporting events or movies that ran over an hour. In comparison, VHS tapes could record for two hours, and JVC would later introduce four-hour tapes.

movie studios to start making tapes in only the VHS format. Though Sony tried, the company failed to convince studios to stick with Betamax.

Betamax had accounted for 41 percent of Sony's income in 1981. But by 1985, Sony had to cut back on Betamax production. It was clear VHS was winning the war of home-use VCRs. In 1988, Sony started producing Betamax for professional use only. Betamax was still popular in that market because video professionals felt it had sharper images than VHS.

Regardless of why experts said VHS won the video format war over Betamax, Morita had his own explanation. He believed if Sony had controlled some of the content—the television shows being taped or the movies being rented—Betamax could have won the format war. The lesson was not lost on him. +

Morita believed Betamax's failure was an important lesson to take into Sony's future.

The compact disc and player changed the music industry—and helped usher in a new era for Sony as an entertainment giant.

MEDIA GIANTS

For Sony, the success with the Walkman took some of the sting out of losing the video format war. Ever since it came out in 1979, the Walkman was the envy of corporations throughout the electronics field. It gave Sony superstar status, despite its setback with Betamax.

Plus, Sony made enough money from the Walkman and other products to allow the company to act on the lessons learned from the Betamax format war. Sony turned its business focus onto the next wave of technology as well as entertainment content, such as music, movies, and television shows.

THE COMPACT DISC

Sony executive Norio Ohga was one of the driving forces behind the development of the compact disc (CD), which engineers from Sony and Philips Electronics worked on together. Philips had proposed the disc be 4.53 inches (11.5 cm) in diameter. At that size, the CD had only 60 minutes of listening time. But Ohga insisted the disc be

RESISTANCE

The music industry did not welcome the CD with open arms. Audiocassettes were popular at the time. So were vinyl records, which music companies had invested in. That meant they had financial incentive to stick with records, rather than release music on CDs. Nevertheless, in October 1982, Billy Joel's *52nd Street* became the first album released on CD. Many others soon followed. In only four years, production of CDs overtook the production of records.

4.8 inches (12 cm) in diameter. That would provide 74 minutes of recording time—enough to listen to Beethoven's *Symphony No. 9* without interruption. The 74-minute CD remains the industry standard to this day.

Under Ohga's leadership, Sony released the world's first music CD in 1982, along with the first CD player. The player was about the size of a VCR. In November 1984, Sony introduced Sony Discman, a portable version.

Fueling the success of Sony's CD technology was its partnership with CBS Records, the label that put out music by such megastars as Michael Jackson, Bruce Springsteen, and

VOICING AN OPINION

Ohga's relationship with Sony began in 1951. Ohga, a student at Tokyo University of the Arts, aspired to be an opera singer. He knew a great deal about audio technology. He wrote a letter to the company, listing ten shortcomings he found with their tape recorders. He said he would advise the school not to buy the tape recorders until the problems were corrected. Ibuka thought Ohga had good suggestions for how to improve the devices. Soon Ohga began attending the company's technical meetings. Ibuka ordered that no tape recorder be put into production without Ohga testing it.

When Ohga graduated from the university in 1953, Morita offered him a job. But Ohga served only as an unpaid consultant for the company, wanting to pursue a career in music instead. Morita spent the next six years recruiting him, believing all along Ohga was the key to the company's future success in the audio world. Ohga finally came on board in April 1959.

Barbra Streisand. Years before, in March 1968, the two companies had formed a joint venture, which Ohga oversaw. Once Sony began marketing CDs in the 1980s, the company's partnership with CBS allowed it to release many popular music artists' albums on CDs. As Sony's CDs became more and more popular, other record companies had to adopt the new technology. There would be no format war this time. It proved what Morita and Ohga had believed all along: owning the content made the difference when it came to selling the technology format.

In January 1988, Sony purchased CBS Records. The deal cost Sony $2 billion. Later, on January 1, 1991, the company was renamed Sony Music Entertainment. At that point, owning a movie studio started making sense to everyone at Sony. In the wake of the Betamax failure,

TRENDSETTER

The Sony Discman fueled the popularity of CDs. The hand-held CD player, complete with headphones, was an instant sensation. It was easy to carry in a jacket pocket and trendy—just like the Walk-man before it. In fact, the Discman was called CD Walk-man in Japan. In 1999, the product's name became CD Walkman worldwide.

Purchasing CBS Records gave Sony access to superstars. In 1993, Norio Ohga, *right*, celebrated with singers, *from left*, Dolly Parton and Barbra Streisand.

one of Morita's goals was for Sony to own a movie company and, more important, the studio's library of films.

Ohga was also determined to make owning a movie company a reality. Like Morita, he strongly believed Sony had to become a multifaceted company and go beyond electronics in order to survive. To him, that meant becoming a global entertainment powerhouse. Music was one aspect of his vision, and the acquisition of CBS Records was paying off. But there was more to be done.

SONY BUYS COLUMBIA

Sony executives looked at many major movie studios, including Paramount and MCA/Universal, as they considered which to buy. Then in the fall of 1988, word came from Hollywood that the Coca-Cola Company was interested in selling its Columbia Pictures studio. Columbia had a library of approximately 3,000 films. It included standout movies such as *Ghostbusters* and *Close Encounters of the Third Kind.*

COLUMBIA'S HISTORY

In purchasing Columbia Pictures, Sony purchased a piece of Hollywood history. Harry and Jack Cohn started CBC Film Sales Corporation in 1919. They changed the name to Columbia Picture Corporation in 1924. The studio really took off when director Frank Capra came to work for it in 1927. He would go on to direct such movies as *It's a Wonderful Life.* The studio also found success with the addition of the Three Stooges to its roster of stars in 1934. The Three Stooges were a comedy act now famous for their slapstick style.

WHAT'S ON TELEVISION?

To Ohga, the hidden treasure in the Columbia Pictures deal was the studio's television shows. "Movies are a studio's marquee, but the money is made in television. I was interested in how many programs they could turn out each month," he said.[1] Ohga thought Columbia's television shows would reap large profits with syndicated reruns and videotape sales.

More attractive were Columbia's television properties, which included approximately 25,000 episodes of some of the most popular television shows ever. *I Dream of Jeannie, Bewitched,* and *The Monkees* were just a few. Columbia also owned popular shows that were on the air at the time, including *Who's the Boss?* and *Designing Women.*

Ohga worked on putting together the deal. After much negotiation, Sony purchased Columbia Pictures on September 28, 1989, for $3.4 billion. By 1991, Columbia Pictures was renamed Sony Pictures Entertainment. The sale prompted a lot of anti-Japanese feelings in Hollywood. Some people feared it meant Japanese companies were trying to take over US institutions. Morita had a different take on the sale. He explained that the purchase deepened the ties between Japan and the United States.

There was another problem as well. Sony had no experience in making movies, so it brought in US movie producers to run the studio. The studio had several hits in its first couple years, including *Basic Instinct* and *Terminator 2.* But losses far outweighed gains. The producers had spent too much on movies that turned out to be flops. Gradually through the years, Sony learned how to better manage the studio's finances. Losses started turning into profits. Movies such as *Jerry Maguire*, *Men in Black*, and the phenomenally successful *Spider-Man*, which made $675 million in two months, helped spin losses into profits. Earnings from video sales also helped with the turnaround.

While Sony battled to make its Columbia Pictures deal profitable, the company was shaken

SHAPING ENTERTAINMENT

Sony now had entertainment content to help sell its technology. But Sony also had an opportunity for its technology to help shape the future of entertainment content. In 1991, Sony built a production center at the Sony Pictures studio to showcase high-definition (HD) technology and computer-aided special effects. Filmmakers, even those from other studios, were invited to experiment with the technology to learn how it could enhance their movies and television programs. The idea was to get Hollywood excited about HD technology, which Sony would soon feature in its televisions, Blu-ray players and discs, and other products.

at its core on November 30, 1993. At age 72, Morita suffered a stroke while playing tennis. The left side of his face and body were paralyzed, and he could not speak. Morita, who had built Sony into a corporate giant and who could talk to business leaders worldwide on a personal level, was left incapacitated. Sony would have to move forward without him. +

As *Time* magazine declared, *Spider-Man* was a smashing success for Sony Pictures in 2002.

Sony's PlayStation game consoles—especially the PS2, launched in 2000—were worldwide hits.

IN THE GAME

Following his stroke, Morita remained Sony chairman, but he was unable to return to work. Ohga ran Sony in his place for a year. Morita officially retired on November 25, 1994, and Ohga became chairman. Ohga's top priority

was to make Sony a dominant force in the world
of entertainment.

Having made inroads in music and movies, the
next frontier was home video games. Ken Kutaragi,
a young engineer at Sony, had been pushing the
company to stake its claim in video games since
the early 1980s. He was convinced video games
had the potential to be a huge profit maker for
Sony. However, hardly anyone at Sony shared
his enthusiasm.

In the mid-1980s, Kutaragi purchased a
Nintendo game console for his young daughter.
He noticed the games were stored on magnetic
cartridges. Kutaragi wondered why Nintendo used
such an unsophisticated storage system with its
advanced gaming product. He felt Sony technology
could greatly improve the Nintendo.

But without support from anyone at Sony,
his ideas were going nowhere. "It was a kind of
snobbery. For people within Sony, the Nintendo
product would have been very embarrassing to make
because it was only a toy," Kutaragi said.[1]

A SONY-NINTENDO COLLABORATION

In 1986, Kutaragi took matters into his own hands. He met with some senior managers at Nintendo, also a Japanese company. He tried convincing them to use Sony's technology to help upgrade their product. The meeting resulted in a deal for the two companies to work together. The only problem was that Kutaragi had no power at Sony to make such a deal. He secretly worked on the project for a while, but Sony's upper management soon learned of the deal. They were furious. Luckily, though, the joint project with Nintendo intrigued Ohga. Instead of

PRESIDENTIAL DECISION

When Morita was sidelined with his stroke in 1993, it left many unanswered questions. The most important was, once Ohga became Sony chairman, who would succeed him as president? Ohga and Morita had never discussed the matter, and now they could not. Ohga took a full year to make a decision.

Sony had always placed a great deal of importance on seniority. But Ohga broke with that tradition and shocked everyone by choosing Nobuyuki Idei to succeed him. Idei leapfrogged over 16 senior Sony executives to the presidency. He was not an engineer. Instead, he impressed Ohga with his leadership skills and desire to maximize Sony's brand while in charge of worldwide advertising and marketing.

Idei took office in March 1995 and made some controversial changes. One was to trim the company's board of directors. He also brought in people from outside the company to be board members.

firing Kutaragi, Ohga eventually gave his approval for the deal to continue.

By 1989, Sony and Nintendo were working on a CD-ROM attachment for the Super Nintendo console. The project was nearly completed in 1991 when the working relationship between the two companies fell apart. They had disagreed about how to share profits. Ohga was infuriated with Nintendo's actions. It only strengthened his resolve to get Sony into the gaming market on its own.

Ohga encouraged Kutaragi to continue his work and develop a game console to rival Nintendo's. Sony even created Sony Computer Entertainment, a subsidiary company, on November 16, 1993, to coordinate its video game business. "I convinced them that computer entertainment would be very important for the future of Sony," Kutaragi recalled.[2]

WORK HARD, PLAY HARDER

Ohga wanted Sony's new game console to have an imaginative name that would instantly speak to consumers. As Kutaragi worked on the project in 1992 and 1993, it finally came to him. People sit at a workstation when on the job. This new console was for not for work, but just the opposite—fun and entertainment. PlayStation was the perfect name.

Ken Kutaragi, the "Father of the PlayStation," led the way for Sony to compete in the video game market.

PLAYSTATION HITS THE MARKET

Sony would not be disappointed with its decision to forge ahead with the creation of a gaming system. By mid-1994, Sony completed work on the PlayStation game console. It was a CD-ROM–based system and featured a chip that could process impressive 3-D graphics. This graphic quality was vital to the console's success.

PlayStation hit stores in Japan in December 1994. In six months, it sold 1 million units. The console swept through Europe and the United States in September 1995. By the end of 1998, PlayStation had sold 50 million units. It accounted for more than 40 percent of Sony's profit. PlayStation's innovative technology brought an end to cartridge-based consoles and launched a new era in the gaming market.

Even as sales of the original PlayStation continued soaring, Sony announced the development of PlayStation 2 (PS2) in early 1999. PS2 arrived in Japanese retail stores in March 2000. It sold just under a million units in three days. The PS2 went beyond playing games. It could also play

THE GAMES PEOPLE PLAY

While developing the original PlayStation, Sony began rounding up independent game designers to create software for its new hardware. They had game designers in Japan ready to submit ideas, and more designers were ready in the United States and Europe. Other game manufacturers were known to be very hard on designers, limiting their creativity. But Sony gave the designers freedom to submit whatever they imagined would make a great game. Sony personnel tested each game before deciding which ones they would ultimately produce for the console.

audio CDs and movie DVDs, expanding its appeal. It was the most technically advanced gaming console of its time.

WINNING EDGE

When it comes to releasing a product in the gaming market, timing is everything. Sony's PlayStation 2 was on retailers' shelves a full year before the next-generation consoles from Nintendo and Microsoft. This gave PS2 a huge head start in sales over its fierce rivals. That, combined with the fact that PS2 was the most technologically advanced console of its time, made it a runaway success. As of January 2012, nearly 155 million PS2s had been sold.

GOING STRONG

When PS2 hit stores in the United States in October 2000, Sony could not make units fast enough. The frenzy confirmed that Kutaragi was a true innovator. It was quite a turn from the days when executives did not respect his ideas about game consoles. "They used to say I was merely lucky with the PlayStation," Kutaragi said.[3] By 2003, Sony controlled 70 percent of the gaming market, and PlayStation and PS2 were responsible for 60 percent of Sony's profits.

Though PS2 was still very popular, gamers pushed Sony to produce PlayStation 3 (PS3). The new console came out in November 2006. PS3 was never as popular as its predecessor, yet it has still sold more than 62 million units.

A major draw for PS3 was that it could play Sony's latest movie format—Blu-ray discs. Sony introduced Blu-ray in Japan in 2003. They then fine-tuned and released it in the United States in 2006. Blu-ray discs provide high-definition video and have the capacity to store more information than DVDs. Rival manufacturers, including Toshiba, challenged Blu-ray with an HD-DVD disc. Microsoft's Xbox 360, a PS3 rival, could play HD-DVDs with a special add-on component. It was another format war. But Blu-ray gained the advantage when Sony released PS3. Toshiba announced in 2008 it would stop making HD-DVD players. Sony claimed victory this time.

In keeping with the "Sony size" tradition, Sony also developed a miniature, portable

VAIO

PS3 is not the only Sony product that can play Blu-ray discs. So can some VAIO computers. VAIO, which stands for Visual Audio Intelligent Organizer, was first launched by Sony in 1996 and includes notebooks, subnotebooks, and desktops. Over the years, Sony's main sales pitch for VAIO computers has been their entertainment value. Top-of-the-line VAIO products now have Blu-ray readers, and some have Blu-ray burners that can record television shows in the high-quality format.

edition of PlayStation. PlayStation Portable (PSP) was approximately the size of a remote control. It played games, music, and movies. When the PSP was released in Japan in December 2004, Sony sold 800,000 units in the first six weeks. PSP reached the United States in spring 2005. In 2007, Sony built an even slimmer, lighter PSP that also had a microphone. For the newest generation of portable, Sony released PlayStation Vita in Japan in December 2011 and in the United States in February 2012.

Fun and games have become a serious business for Sony. They helped the company compete in the new millennium, just as Kutaragi predicted. +

PlayStation Portable, first released in 2004, makes gaming "Sony sized."
Here, two units play head to head.

Former CEO and president Howard Stringer, *right*, and his successor,
Kazuo Hirai, would lead Sony through difficult times.

REBOOTING THE DREAM

The end of the twentieth century was a very difficult time for the Sony Corporation. It lost both of its cofounders. The two men were the heart and soul of Sony. Together, they had set a high standard for innovation, product marketing, and business expertise as they built the company from its humble beginnings.

On December 19, 1997, Masaru Ibuka died at age 89. He is credited with making Japan's electronics business what it is today. Sony chairman Ohga said of Ibuka's death,

> *To us, the passing of Masaru Ibuka means that we have lost that which supports our spirits and hearts. But we will continue our efforts to ensure that the philosophy that Masaru Ibuka left with us always remains alive at the core of Sony.*[1]

More than 1,500 people attended a company funeral for Ibuka. With Morita still unable to speak from his 1993 stroke, Ohga asked Morita's wife, Yoshiko, to address mourners at the funeral. She gave a heartfelt tribute to the man who cofounded the electronics giant with her husband.

The Sony family was equally grief stricken when Akio Morita died on October 3, 1999, at age 78. Morita was known worldwide

"Masaru Ibuka was a person of an entirely different dimension. In the middle of the desolation of post-war Japan, he set out a grand aim in the founding prospectus of the company, and then made unending efforts to create a company that could realize this fine goal. Every single employee from Akio Morita on down worked to achieve Masaru Ibuka's dream."[2]

—*Norio Ohga, shortly after Ibuka's death in 1997*

for his ability to develop long-lasting and mutually beneficial business relationships. His image even graced the cover of *Time* magazine. Peter Peterson, a prominent American businessman and investment banker, once said of Morita,

> *When it came time for Akio [Morita] to do business in the United States, whether it was joint ventures or licensing or whatever, he could pick up the phone and talk to almost any businessman in America. . . . Akio knew these people at the human level, at the personal level. . . . Therefore when he called, people listened.*[3]

ON A DOWNHILL SLIDE

Ohga remained chairman of Sony until he retired in 2003. Nobuyuki Idei then became chairman. But Idei's time as Sony's leader was a rocky one. He was not able to help Sony regain its title as the electronics industry's grand innovator.

The company was regularly losing out to visionary products developed by Apple and Samsung. Idei never saw Apple's iPod coming. Sony was also late to pick up on trends such as flat-screen televisions, cell phones, and digital cameras. A hit product such as the Walkman or a compact disc player had not come from the company in some time. Instead, Sony had to play catch-up with the latest products other companies were developing. It was tarnishing the Sony reputation as a market leader. By 2005, Sony's profits were down. Though Idei was trying to turn things around, stockholders were losing patience.

Idei retired in June 2005, making way for former CBS president Sir Howard Stringer to become Sony chairman and CEO. He was the first foreign-born person to run a Japanese-based electronics company. He had previously held many positions with the company. In 1997, he became president of Sony Corporation of America. He had also been chairman of Sony Pictures Entertainment. As chairman of Sony Corporation, though, he had a big challenge ahead of him.

Stringer focused his efforts on restructuring Sony and gaining back some lost territory in the market. It was not easy. Even Sony's television division lost money from 2003 to 2011—roughly

SONY'S KNIGHT

Howard Stringer was born in Wales in 1942 and moved to the United States in 1965. He holds dual citizenship in the United States and Great Britain. His many honors include being knighted by Great Britain's Queen Elizabeth II in July 2000. Stringer had spent 30 years as a broadcast executive at CBS, including four years as producer of the *CBS Evening News with Dan Rather.*

$8.5 billion. The losses are expected to continue through 2013. The problem: upstart electronics companies were driving prices too low.

Sony was also losing out to Apple's iPod and iTunes Music Store, which ushered in the era of digital music—and the end of the popularity of CDs. Sony and Apple were working at the same time to develop a device to download music. "[Apple CEO] Steve Jobs figured it out, we figured it out, we didn't execute," Stringer explained. "The music guys didn't want to see the CD go away."[4]

Despite these setbacks, it appeared as though the company was headed toward a profitable year in 2011. Stringer anticipated a $2 billion operating profit. But then something happened that affected not only Sony but the entire country of Japan.

NATURAL DISASTERS STRIKE

On March 11, 2011, a 9.0-magnitude earthquake rumbled through eastern Japan. A highly

HACKED

Sony launched PlayStation Network (PSN), an interactive, online network for PlayStation users, in 2006. But it and Sony Online Entertainment, Sony's online gaming network, was hacked in mid-April 2011, adding to Sony's woes of a disastrous year. The network was down for about a month, affecting 100 million users. Users' personal information was compromised, but PSN returned with new security measures and eventually added 3 million more members.

The 2011 earthquake and tsunami caused much destruction throughout Japan, including Sony's warehouse near Sendai port.

destructive tsunami quickly followed. The natural disasters devastated much of Japan, and Sony experienced its share. Sony plants were damaged and had to be temporarily closed. Production stopped on many items. The company's gains suddenly turned into a $3.1 billion loss.

Even after the Japanese earthquake and tsunami, more disasters struck Sony worldwide. On August 8, 2011, a Sony factory in England burned down during civil unrest in the streets of London. That was followed by massive flooding in Thailand in October 2011. The flooding severely damaged one of Sony's major plants, forcing long delays in the release of four new compact digital cameras.

REGAINING GROUND

Despite its tough times, Sony still had more than 2,000 different products coming out of its 41 factories in 2011. Today, it has a workforce of 168,000 people. Stringer also positioned the company to be a player in the smartphone market. In February 2012, Sony bought out Sony Ericsson, its Swedish partner in the mobile phone business. Sony's goal is to aggressively compete with Apple's iPhone by creating an innovative smartphone of its own. "We can more rapidly and more widely offer consumer smartphones, laptops, tablets and televisions that seamlessly connect with one another and open up new worlds of online entertainment," Stringer said of the opportunity.[5]

In April 2012, Stringer retired as Sony president and CEO. Stringer's protégé, Kazuo Hirai, took his place. He began his career at Sony in 1984, holding numerous executive positions at the company, including chairman of the computer entertainment division. Hirai had revitalized Sony's PlayStation division in 2010, turning a profit after four consecutive years of losses. He is also leading efforts to connect Sony devices and content under the umbrella of the Sony Entertainment Network. With this development, soon all Sony devices will be able to access all Sony content. For example, people with Sony tablets will have special access to exclusive footage of Sony television shows or movies. Hirai said only now is the hardware powerful enough to bring such content to televisions, computers, tablets, and smartphones.

TELECOMMUNICATIONS

In 2001, Sony jumped into the global cell phone market. Sony combined its electronics know-how with Ericsson, one of the world's largest mobile phone manufacturers. The joint venture, Sony Ericsson, produced an assortment of camera and music phones that dazzled consumers—until the iPhone came along in 2007. Then Sony Ericsson started struggling. Sony Ericsson phones were not integrated with other Sony products, such as tablets, televisions, and computers. So, Sony bought out Sony Ericsson in early 2012 to take full control of the company and steer it in new directions. Sony Ericsson became Sony Mobile Communications.

Sony plans to use phones to link Sony content—including games, music, and movies—with its other electronic devices. Sony officials believe the company needs a strong presence in telecommunications to compete in today's consumer electronics market. Sony points to its competitor, Samsung, as an example of how telecommunications can affect the bottom line. Samsung nets nearly half its profits from sales of telecommunication devices. Sony believes it can do the same by adding a smartphone to its product line. By buying out Sony Ericsson, Sony seems primed to be competitive in the smartphone arena.

A NEW PAGE

Sony jumped into the tablet market in 2011, intent on surpassing Apple's iPad. Sony's Tablet S came out in September. It is about the size of an iPad, but its design makes it lighter and easier to hold. November brought the Tablet P, a small dual-screen device that can fit into a purse. It opens like a book. When held vertically, its two screens show two facing pages, like a book spread. Held horizontally, the bottom screen becomes a keyboard, and the top becomes an e-mail window.

When he was named president and CEO, Hirai said,

The path we must take is clear. To drive the growth of our core electronics businesses— primarily digital imaging, smart mobile, and games; to turn around the television business; and to accelerate the innovation that enables us to create new business domains.[6]

To that end, Sony is working on a long list of new imaginative gadgetry. There is one project that seems right in line with Sony's tradition of innovation. It's an ultralow-power, 3-D television set. It requires no glasses to view, and it has better resolution than anything ever to hit the market. It is totally new technology—innovation the Sony way. +

Stretching from its headquarters in Tokyo to around the globe, Sony strives to achieve its innovative vision in the years to come.

TIMELINE

1908	1921	1946
Masaru Ibuka is born on April 11 in Nikko City, Japan.	Akio Morita is born on January 26 in Nagoya, Japan.	On May 7, Ibuka and Morita launch Tokyo Telecommunications Engineering Corporation, which eventually becomes Sony.

1960	1968	1975
Sony releases the mini-television in May.	Sony Trinitron debuts in October.	Sony's Betamax, the first VCR, goes on sale on May 10.

1950	1955	1960
Ibuka and Morita introduce Japan's first tape recorder in January.	Tokyo Telecommunications Engineering Corporation releases Japan's first transistor radio in August.	Sony Corporation of America is founded on February 15.

1979	1982	1988
Sony's Walkman hits retail stores on July 1.	Sony releases the world's first music CD and CD player.	Sony purchases CBS Records in January.

TIMELINE

1989	1993	1994
Sony buys Columbia Pictures on September 28.	Sony chairman Morita suffers a stroke on November 30 and becomes incapacitated.	Morita retires and Norio Ohga takes over as Sony chairman.

2000	2005	2006
PlayStation 2 debuts in the United States in October.	Sir Howard Stringer becomes Sony chairman in June.	Sony releases Blu-ray in the United States.

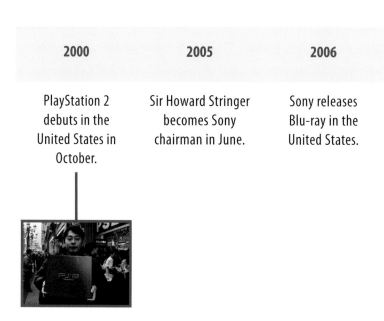

1994	1997	1999
PlayStation hits the market in Japan in December.	Masaru Ibuka dies at age 89 on December 19.	Akio Morita dies at age 78 on October 3.

2011	2012	2012
Sony releases Tablet S and Tablet P to compete with Apple's iPad.	PlayStation Vita is released in the United States in February.	Kazuo Hirai becomes Sony president and CEO in April.

ESSENTIAL FACTS

CREATORS

Masaru Ibuka (April 11, 1908–December 19, 1997)

Akio Morita (January 26, 1921–October 3, 1999)

DATE LAUNCHED

May 7, 1946

CHALLENGES

Sony literally had to be built from the ground up in economically devastated, post–World War II Japan. In the company's early days, founders Masaru Ibuka and Akio Morita had to convince cash-strapped Japanese buyers that they needed the electronic devices the company was producing. Once they made inroads in Japan, Ibuka and Morita worked hard to get their products out to the rest of the world. Driven to succeed, they developed relationships first in the United States and then in other countries to distribute, display, and sell Sony's electronic goods outside Japan. Along the way, they had to dispel the notion that Japanese products were of low quality and poorly made.

SUCCESSES

Sony's drive for innovation has led to the development of countless life-changing products, including tape recorders, transistor radios, mini-televisions, Trinitron color televisions, the Walkman, VCRs, videocassettes, CDs and CD players, camcorders, PlayStation consoles, DVD players, and Blu-ray players.

IMPACT ON SOCIETY

Through its groundbreaking technology, Sony gave consumers worldwide the most advanced electronic products for professional and home use. In addition, by making small, lightweight, easy-to-carry devices such as mini-televisions and the Walkman, Sony launched the microelectronics industry.

QUOTE

"There is nothing more pitiable than a man who can't or doesn't dream. Dreams give direction and purpose to life, without which life would be mere drudgery."

—*Masaru Ibuka*

GLOSSARY

capital
Money or funding for business operations or expansion.

digital
Involving or relating to the use of computer technology.

entrepreneur
A person who starts a business.

format
A particular form of technology.

hardware
The physical components that make up a technology device.

market research
The analysis of data used to determine a product's appeal to particular customers.

microelectronics
A branch of electronics that deals with the miniaturization of electronic circuits, components, and consumer products.

patent
Exclusive rights to an invention, granted by the government to the inventor.

prototype
The original or model on which something is based or formed.

reel-to-reel tape recorder
An audio recording and playback machine that uses magnetic tape held on a reel.

seniority
>   Superior status or rank attained by serving a long period of time in a company.

smartphone
>   A mobile phone with computerlike features including e-mail, Internet, and a personal organizer.

software
>   The programs used to direct the operations of a computer.

stock market
>   A market where stocks and bonds are traded or exchanged.

subsidiary
>   A company under the control of another.

tablet
>   A small rectangular computer that is extremely thin and light.

vacuum tube
>   A hollow glass cylinder used for processing electric signals in electronic devices, including tape recorders, televisions, and radios.

ADDITIONAL RESOURCES

SELECTED BIBLIOGRAPHY

Buchholz, Todd G. *New Ideas from Dead CEOs: Lasting Lessons from the Corner Office.* New York: HarperCollins, 2007. Print.

Hamel, Gary. *Leading the Revolution: How to Thrive in Turbulent Times by Making Innovation a Way of Life.* New York: Plume, 2002. Print.

Lardner, James. *Fast Forward: Hollywood, the Japanese, and the VCR Wars.* New York: Norton, 1987. Print.

Nathan, John. *Sony: A Private Life.* New York: Mariner, 2001. Print.

Ohga, Norio. *Doing It Our Way: A Sony Memoir.* Tokyo: International House of Japan, 2008. Print.

FURTHER READINGS

Bridgman, Roger. *Eyewitness: Electronics.* London: Dorling Kindersley, 2000. Print.

Chang, Se-Jin. *Sony vs. Samsung: The Inside Story of the Electronics Giants' Battle for Global Supremacy.* Hoboken, NJ: Wiley, 2008. Print.

Luh, Shu Shin. *Business the Sony Way.* New York: Wiley, 2003. Print.

WEB LINKS

To learn more about Sony, visit ABDO Publishing Company online at **www.abdopublishing.com**. Web sites about Sony are featured on our Book Links page. These links are routinely monitored and updated to provide the most current information available.

PLACES TO VISIT

PlayStation Lounge
Sony Store
550 Madison Avenue
New York, NY 10022
212-833-8800
http://www.store.sony.com
Located in the flagship Sony store in Sony Tower, the PlayStation
Lounge features all sorts of new games for people to play and test out.

Sony Pictures Studios
10202 W. Washington Boulevard
Culver City, CA 90232
310-244-6926
http://www.sonypicturesstudiostours.com
Some of the best-known movies and television shows have been
filmed at Sony Picture Studios. People can tour the famous lot and
learn about movie and television history.

Sony Tower and Sony Wonder Technology Lab
550 Madison Avenue
New York, NY 10022
212-833-8100
http://sonywondertechlab.com
Sony Wonder Technology Lab is located next to Sony Tower. This
engaging technology and entertainment museum has numerous
hands-on exhibits.

SOURCE NOTES

CHAPTER 1. A SOUND IDEA

1. Akio Morita, with Edwin M. Reingold and Mitsuko Shimomura. *Made in Japan: Akio Morita and Sony.* New York: E. P. Dutton, 1986. Print. 79.

2. William Lidwell and Gerry Manacsa. *Deconstructing Product Design: Exploring the Form, Function, Usability, Sustainability, and Commercial Success of 100 Amazing Productions.* Beverly, MA: Rockport, 2011. Print. 204.

CHAPTER 2. BORN TO INVENT

1. John Nathan. *Sony: The Private Life.* New York: Houghton Mifflin, 1999. Print. 7.

2. Ibid. 18.

CHAPTER 3. RISING FROM THE RUINS

1. John Nathan. *Sony: The Private Life.* New York: Houghton Mifflin, 1999. Print. 22.

2. Akio Morita, with Edwin M. Reingold and Mitsuko Shimomura. *Made in Japan: Akio Morita and Sony.* New York: E. P. Dutton, 1986. Print. 51.

3. "The Founding Prospectus." *Sony Global.* Sony Corporation, 2012. Web. 29 Mar. 2012.

4. John Nathan. *Sony: The Private Life.* New York: Houghton Mifflin, 1999. Print. 26.

5. Ibid. 26.

6. Akio Morita, with Edwin M. Reingold and Mitsuko Shimomura. *Made in Japan: Akio Morita and Sony.* New York: E. P. Dutton, 1986. Print. 57.

CHAPTER 4. SMALL WONDER

1. Akio Morita, with Edwin M. Reingold and Mitsuko Shimomura. *Made in Japan: Akio Morita and Sony.* New York: E. P. Dutton, 1986. Print. 64.

2. Ibid. 70.

3. Ibid.

CHAPTER 5. A BETTER TELEVISION

1. Jeff Yang. "How Steve Jobs 'Out-Japanned' Japan." *SFGate.* Hearst Communications, Inc., 28 Jan. 2011. Web. 29 Mar. 2012.

2. "Chapter 10: Sony Corporation of America." *Sony Global,* Sony Corporation. 2012. Web. 29 Mar. 2012.

3. "Chapter 14: The Aiborne VTR." *Sony Global,* Sony Corporation. 2012. Web. 29 Mar. 2012.

CHAPTER 6. VIDEO WAR

1. "Chapter 1: The Video Cassette Tape." *Sony Global,* Sony Corporation. 2012. Web. 29 Mar. 2012.

2. Ibid.

3. "Early Sony Betamax Commercial plus Crazy Eddie Spot." 1978. *Google Videos.* Web. 12 Apr. 2012.

CHAPTER 7. MEDIA GIANTS

1. John Nathan. *Sony: The Private Life.* New York: Houghton Mifflin, 1999. Print. 186.

SOURCE NOTES CONTINUED

CHAPTER 8. IN THE GAME

1. Gary Hamel. *Leading the Revolution: How to Thrive in Turbulent Times by Making Innovation a Way of Life.* New York: Plume, 2002. Print. 172.

2. Ibid. 174.

3. "Ken Kutaragi: Sony Computer Entertainment." *Bloomberg Businessweek*. Bloomberg, 13 Jan. 2003. Web. 29 Mar. 2012.

CHAPTER 9. REBOOTING THE DREAM

1. "Masaru Ibuka: 1908–1997." *Sony Global*. Sony Corporation, 6 Jan. 1998. Web. 29 Mar. 2012.

2. Ibid.

3. John Nathan. *Sony: The Private Life.* New York: Houghton Mifflin, 1999. Print. 77.

4. Bryan Gruley and Cliff Edwards. "What Is Sony Now?" *Bloomberg Businessweek*. Bloomberg, 17 Nov. 2011. Web. 29 Mar. 2012.

5. Tarmo Virki. "Sony Buys Ericsson out of Mobile Phone Venture." *Reuters*. Thomson Reuters, 27 Oct. 2011. Web. 29 Mar. 2012.

6. Yoko Kubota and Liana B. Baker. "Sony Names New CEO." *Toronto Sun*. Sun Media Corp., 1 Feb. 2012. Web. 29 Mar. 2012.

INDEX

INDEX CONTINUED

ABOUT THE AUTHOR

Robert Grayson is an award-winning former daily newspaper reporter and the author of books for young adults. Throughout his journalism career, Grayson has written stories on professional athletes, arts and entertainment, business, politics, and pets. His articles have appeared in national and regional publications, including *Yankees Magazine* and the NBA's *HOOP* magazine. He has written biographies of environmental activists and sports figures as well as books about animals in the military, animal performers, law enforcement, and major historical events.

PHOTO CREDITS

Kurita Kaku/Gamma-Rapho/Getty Images, cover; Neal Ulevich/ AP Images, 6; Sony/AP Images, 13; Bettmann/Corbis/AP Images, 15; Kyodo News/AP Images, 16; MPI/Getty Images, 21; Charles P. Gorry/AP Images, 25; Tsugufumi Matsumoto/AP Images, 26; AP Images, 33, 49; Yoshikazu Tsuno/AFP/Getty Images, 35; MC/ AP Images, 36, 97 (top), 99 (top); Kim Kyung-Hoon/Reuters, 40, 91; John Roderick/AP Images, 45; SSPL/Getty Images, 46, 59, 96; Dave Pickoff/AP Images, 55; Lennox Mclendon/AP Images, 56; Susumi Takahashi/Bettmann/Corbis/AP Images, 65; Katsumi Kasahara/AP Images, 66; Osamu Honda/AP Images, 70, 97 (bottom); Chiaki Tsukumo/AP Images, 75; Toshifumi Kitamura/ AFP/Getty Images, 76, 98; Susan Goldman/Bloomberg/Getty Images, 80; Koji Sasahara/AP Images, 85; Kazuhiro Nogi/AFP/ Getty Images, 86, 99 (bottom); Koichi Kamoshida/Getty Images, 95